This book belongs to:

Secret Colors

by Martin Kleppmann and Mitch Seymour

Text copyright © 2022 Martin Kleppmann
Illustrations copyright © 2022 Mitch Seymour

All rights reserved. This book or any portion thereof may not be reproduced or used in any manner whatsoever without the express written permission of the publisher except for the use of brief quotations in a book review.

First printing, 2022.

Round Robin Publishing
www.roundrobin.pub

 *hello@roundrobin.pub*

Secret Colors

Written by Martin Kleppmann
Illustrated by Mitch Seymour

The rabbits lived in a beautiful forest. It was autumn, and the leaves of the trees shone in the morning sun in all shades of gold, red, yellow, orange, and brown.

Two little rabbits, Emi and Moriko, stopped to admire the leaves on their way to school.

They wondered at the bright red leaves of the maple and marveled at the deep orange leaves of the mountain ash along with its red berries.

But most of all, Emi loved the golden yellow glow of the river birch, and Moriko agreed.

Because rabbits are Secretive Animals, they decided to tell nobody else about their favorite color.

When the rabbits arrived at school, they sat in their seats and the teacher read the morning announcements.

"The Autumn Dance is this Saturday!" she announced. "Everyone, please find a very special bunny to bring with you."

The classroom began to hum with who-will-you-brings and what-will-you-wears until the teacher said "quiet, please!"

It became clear that all further conversations would need to happen by passing notes.

Being a nosy little rabbit, Moriko wrote Emi a note that said,

"which bunny will you ask to the dance?"

Since they sat on opposite sides of the classroom, several bunnies had to pass along Moriko's note before it arrived with Emi.

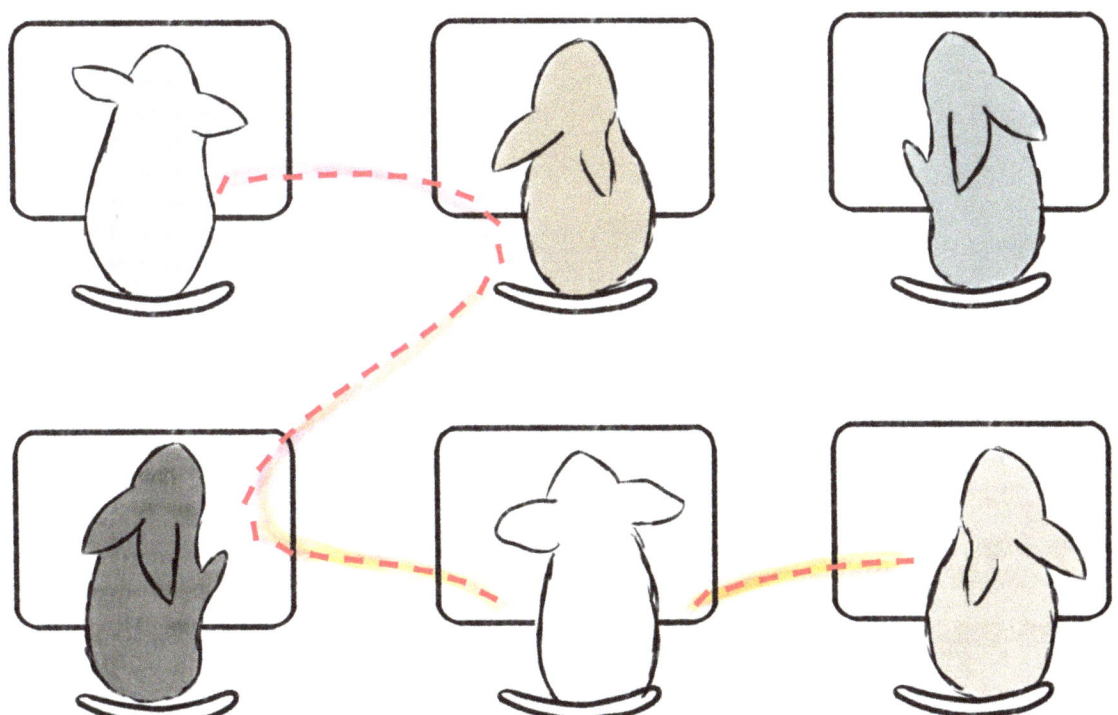

Emi didn't mind sharing her plans with Moriko, but she knew that some of the other bunnies might peek at the note as it was passed around.

Then, Emi had a bright idea. She took out her paints and brushes, which were in her bag for the arts class later in the day, and on her note she wrote four different answers

in four different colors.

I want to ask Ren, she wrote in

the red of the maple.

I want to ask Nori, she wrote in

the orange of the mountain ash.

I want to ask Sora, she wrote in

the yellow of the river birch.

I want to ask Kumi, she wrote in

the green of the pine.

Then, Emi passed the note with the four differently colored answers across the classroom.

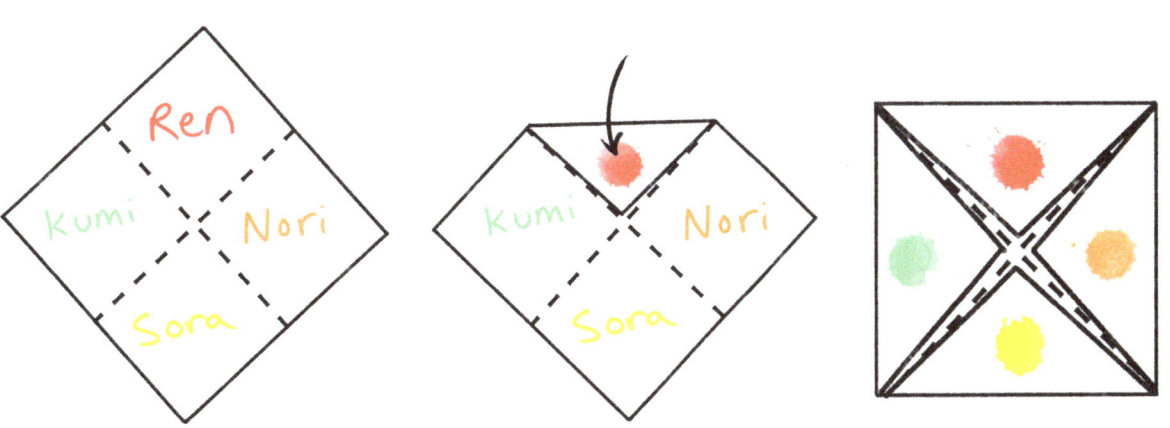

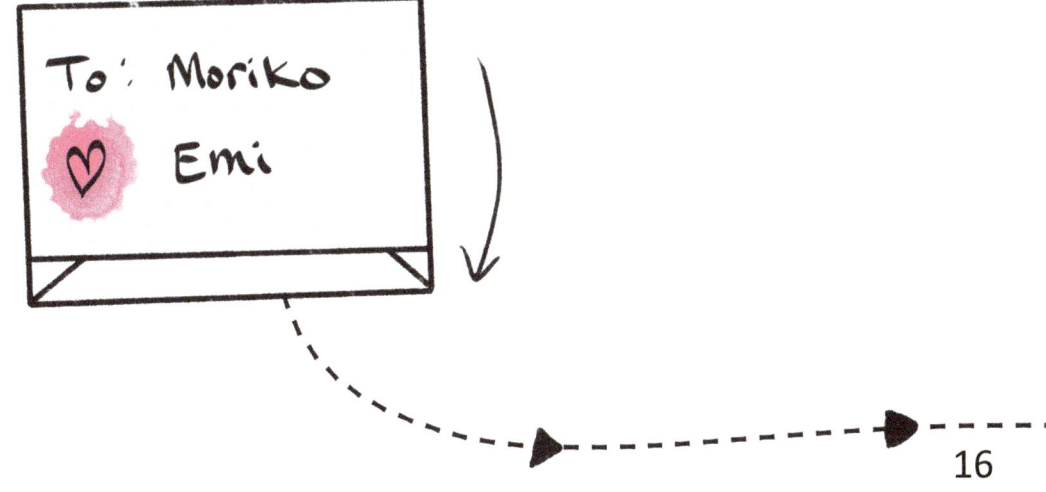

Here's the trick: only one of the answers that Emi wrote was true, and the other answers were lies! But nobody would know which is which — except for Moriko, who knew Emi's favorite color.

Any other bunnies who peeked at the note would have no idea,

because they did not know Emi's favorite color.

Emi hummed a little song to describe her clever scheme.

A tisket, a tasket

A green and yellow basket

I wrote a letter to my friend

And now I need to pass it

I'll pass it, I'll pass it

By all the nosy rabbits

And even if they take a peek

They should never grasp it

Encryption, encryption

A suitable description

For what we did, when we hid

The message in plain vision

A few minutes later, Sakura passed Emi a note. Sakura also wanted to know who Emi was planning on asking to the Autumn Dance.

Unfortunately, Emi and Sakura had not talked about their favorite colors before, and so Emi could not use the same trick as with Moriko.

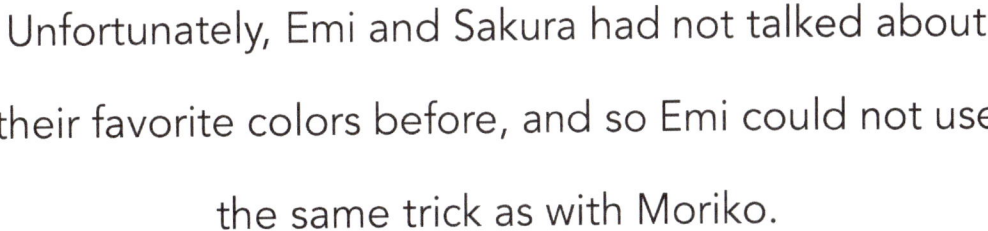

If Emi were to tell Sakura in a note what the true color was, then the other prying rabbits would peek and figure it out.

She knew that they needed some way of creating a shared color, known only to the two of them and nobody else. Then she could write the true answer in their shared color, and the lies in other colors.

But was this possible?

Then Emi remembered the time when she and Sakura made a carrot cake for the class last spring.

They followed a well-known recipe for carrot cake, but then each rabbit added their own secret ingredient for fun.

Sakura's secret ingredient

Emi's secret ingredient

The carrot cake was a hit, and everyone asked for the recipe. But even though the other rabbits knew most of the ingredients...

They couldn't figure out how exactly the cake was made, since both Emi and Sakura had added their own secret ingredients.

This gave Emi an idea. Instead of a secret carrot cake recipe, this time Emi and Sakura would make a **shared color** that nobody else would know. She got her set of paints ready.

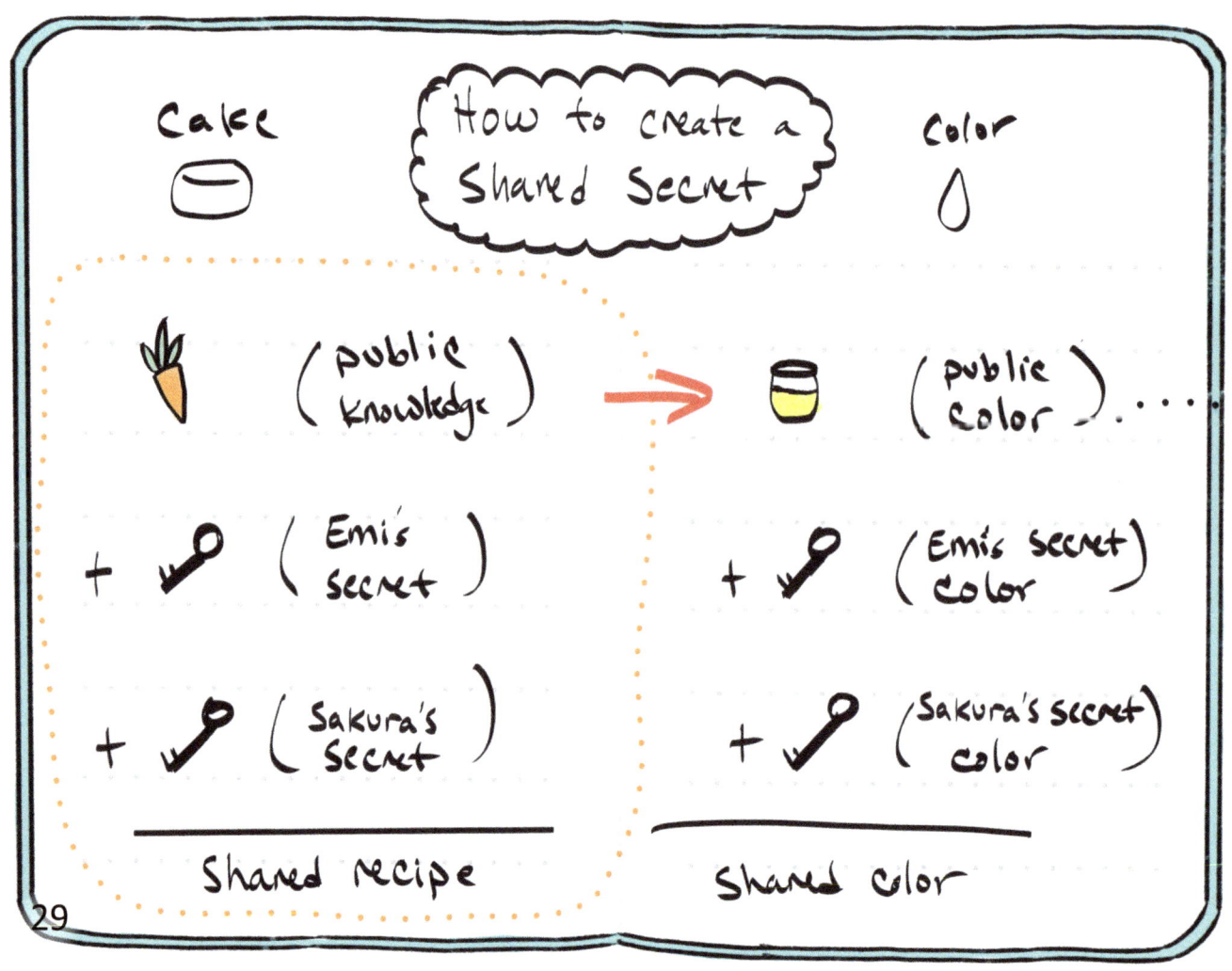

First, Emi needed a starting color. She chose the pale yellow color of the sycamore tree, which dropped its leaves right in front of the classroom window. She then wrote on her note that Sakura should use the same pale yellow as her starting color.

It wouldn't matter if the other bunnies figured out the starting color, because it's not the same as their shared color.

Next, Emi and Sakura each picked a secret color that they wouldn't share with anyone, not even each other.

Emi chose sourwood red,

While Sakura decided to use robin egg blue
(a beautiful greenish blue color).

Emi then mixed her secret color with the starting color, stirred well, and filled the mixture into a little jar.

Likewise, Sakura mixed her own secret color with the starting color and poured the paint into a jar.

Then they passed the jars to each other across the classroom.
Any of the other bunnies could see the contents of the jars,
but it didn't matter.

When Emi received Sakura's jar, she added some more of her own secret color to the mixture.

Similarly, when Sakura got the mixture from Emi, she added her own secret color.

They stirred well, and guess what? Now both of them had exactly the same mixture!

Both contained the starting color, some of Emi's secret color, and some of Sakura's secret color.

Even though Emi never told anyone else her secret color, and neither had Sakura, both of them had ended up with the same shared color.

And what about the other nosy bunnies? They saw the starting color and the contents of the jars that were passed around, but from this they could not figure out what Emi and Sakura's shared color was.

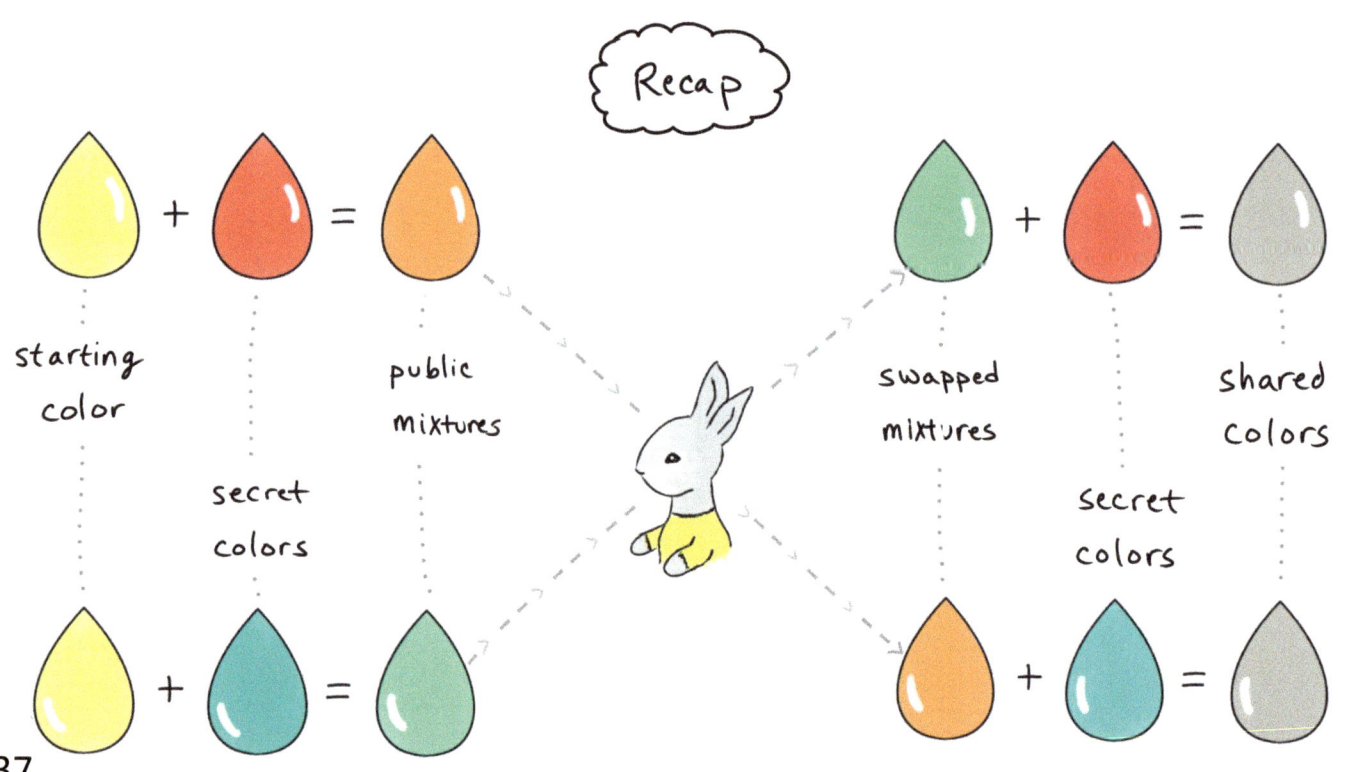

Now Emi could use the same trick as she had done before with Moriko. She wrote four different answers in four different colors.

The true answer was written using the paint she and Sakura had mixed, while the lies were written in different colors.

And because Sakura knew the shared color, she could tell which of the answers was true.

Now Moriko and Sakura knew that Emi wanted to ask Sora to the dance, but the other nosy rabbits were left wondering.

Until the next Saturday, when they all went to the Autumn Dance…

Appendix
For older readers who want to know more

We hope you enjoyed the story of Emi, Moriko, Sakura, and their secret messages. But did you know that computers and phones actually work in a similar way? Every time you send a message to your friend using the internet, the computer or phone uses similar tricks to make sure that only your friend can read the message, and nobody else.

The technical name for this is **encryption,** as you already heard in Emi's song. The basic idea of encryption is that you have a **secret key** that is used to scramble the message you send. The secret message you want to send is called the **plaintext,** and the result of encrypting the plaintext is called **ciphertext.** Somebody else who also knows that secret key can **decrypt** the ciphertext to get back the plaintext, but to anyone who doesn't know the secret key, the ciphertext is just nonsense. When the ciphertext is passed via the nosy bunnies, that's like when a message is sent over the **Internet.**

In our story, Emi and Moriko's favorite color — the yellow of the river birch — is their secret key. Their ciphertext consists of four answers, of which only one is true. If someone who doesn't know the favorite color reads the message, all four answers are equally likely, and so they don't find out the true answer.

But isn't it impractical to write out one true answer along with several lies?

Correct, and real encryption doesn't actually work that way. Instead, real encryption usually works one letter at a time: for example, A gets replaced with

F, B gets replaced with Q, and so on. The encrypted message then looks like LIPXBFEOAGWOCDJMHJFKYHGBYSGRTUIZNKL or something similarly unreadable. For this story, we wanted to use colors, and the trick of having one true answer and several lies made that possible.

To be more technical: say we have a note containing one true answer and three lies, so the true answer is one of four possibilities. To make them short, we could also call those possibilities 0, 1, 2, and 3. Computer scientists like to use binary to write those numbers as 00, 01, 10, and 11. In this case, we say that we want to encrypt a two-bit message (which means that each of those binary numbers is two digits long). As long as there are at least four possibilities for the secret key color, we can encrypt the two-bit message perfectly. If our message is longer than two bits, then things get more complicated.

Isn't Emi giving away that the true answer must be one of the four?

You're right: when nosy rabbits peek at the note with the four names (Ren, Nori, Sora, Kumi), they know that the true answer must be one of those four. They can be sure that Emi is not asking Akari, for example. This gives away some information about the plaintext to the nosy rabbits.

In real encryption, where the message is scrambled one letter at a time, we don't have this problem. However, there is a different problem instead: anybody peeking at the encrypted message can count how many letters there are. If there are three letters, and Ren is the only bunny with a three-letter name in the class, you might guess that Ren is the correct answer. Or if you can guess that the message is either "yes" or "no", then you can tell which one it was, depending on whether the ciphertext has two or three letters. It's difficult to really make sure that the ciphertext does not give away any information at all about the plaintext.

What if the rabbits want to send each other more than one message?

Then they have to be careful. Let's say that after asking Emi who she's inviting to the dance, Moriko asks Emi what her favorite flavor of ice cream is. Emi again answers by writing her true favorite flavor in her favorite color, and by writing lies in three different colors.

But maybe there are other bunnies in the class who already know Emi's favorite ice cream flavor — it's not exactly a great secret. If they peek at the message, they will know which one of the answers is true, and therefore they can figure out which color is Emi and Moriko's favorite. And using that information, they can now decrypt the original message about who Emi is inviting to the dance. Now the original message is no longer secret!

This problem happened because Emi and Moriko used the same secret key color for several messages, but the trick of writing one true answer and several lies is only safe if the secret key is only used once (experts call this a "one-time pad"). To be safe, the bunnies either have to work out a new secret color for every single message they want to send, or they need to use a more advanced encryption method that allows a key to be used several times. The details of how this works will have to remain a topic for another time.

When passing around jars of paint, couldn't the other rabbits figure out the shared color?

You're right: when you mix paints together, you can often guess what paints went into the mixture. For example, if you mix yellow and blue, you usually get green. Therefore, if you know that yellow was mixed with some secret color, and the result is green, then the secret color was probably blue. With a bit of trial and error, you could probably work out the exact shade of blue. If you can figure out what other color went into a mixture, then Emi and Sakura's scheme of passing jars of paint is no longer safe: the other rabbits will be able to work out the secret colors that were mixed together, and therefore they will also be able to make their own jar of Emi and Sakura's shared color, and decrypt the message that uses this shared color as its secret key.

In real encryption, instead of mixing paints, we use a mathematical calculation that mixes very long numbers together in a way that makes the numbers impossible to separate again. In real life, Emi and Sakura's swapping of jars is done by sending those long numbers over the Internet. This particular approach is called **Diffie-Hellman Key Exchange** (invented by three computer scientists called Whitfield Diffie, Martin Hellman, and Ralph Merkle).

Visit **https://roundrobin.pub/pages/secret-colors**
to learn how can we do this with numbers instead of paints,
and for more resources about cryptography.

Martin is a computer scientist. He teaches students at an old university in Cambridge (England), and he has written a thick computing book with a wild boar on the front. He is also trying to make computers better and more secure for groups of people who need to work together.

Mitch is a software engineer and the founder of Round Robin Publishing. He has written and illustrated other books, as well, including one about data streams and cute little otters (Gently Down the Stream). He is inspired by his two daughters, Isabelle and Chloe, and wants to make technology fun for beginners of all ages.

www.gentlydownthe.stream

www.ingramcontent.com/pod-product-compliance
Ingram Content Group UK Ltd.
Pitfield, Milton Keynes, MK11 3LW, UK
UKHW052121230426
12049UKWH00010BA/143